Welsh Shipwrecks
In Camera

by
Phil Carradice

QUOTES LIMITED

MCMXCIII

Published by Quotes Limited
Whittlebury, England

Typeset in Plantin by
Key Composition, Northampton, England

Pictures Lithographed by
South Midlands Lithoplates Limited, Luton, England

Printed by Busiprint Limited
Buckingham, England

Bound by WBC Bookbinders Limited

ISBN 0 86023 600 5

Acknowledgements

Particular and special thanks must go to Ted Goddard, Tom Bennett and Carl Smith for their help in the researching of this book; also thanks to Richard Phillips and the staff of Cardiff Central Library, the staff of Pembrokeshire County Library (Haverfordwest) and the Pembrokeshire Records Office. Special thanks go to Iain Boothe, Jim Arnold, Mr & Mrs J. V. Reeves, Peter Williams, Gill Mace of the RNLI, Jim Roberts, Martin Delosso, Mrs A. Hughes and Alun Williams. As ever, Trudy McNally deserves particular appreciation, not only for typing the MS but also for offering constructive criticism of the text.

Key to Photographers

GAS	Gwynedd Archives Services
NMM	National Maritime Museum
JR	Jim Roberts
IB	Iain Boothe
PC	Phil Carradice
AMC	Andrew Carradice
WT	*Western Telegraph*
JV	J V Reeves
RE/CE	Roy & Christine Evans
AW	Alun Williams
WIMM	Welsh Industrial Maritime Museum
KD	Ken Daniels
RAF	RAF Brawdy
LB	Lyn Bryant
PCL	Pembrokeshire County Library
RNLI	Royal National Lifeboat Institution
TG	Ted Goddard
AH	Mrs A Hughes
MLS	Mumbles Lifeboat Station

Bibliography

Tom Bennet *Shipwrecks Around Wales* Vol I and Vol II, Happy Fish, 1992

Phil Carradice *The Book of Pembroke Dock* Barracuda, 1991

G. M. & R. C. Davies *The Loss of HMS Montague* privately published, 1981

G. M. Dixon *For Those in Peril: The Lifeboatmen* Minimax Books, 1981

George Edmunds *The Gower Coast* Regional Publications, 1979

Bernard Edwards *The Grey Widow Maker* Robert Hale, 1990

Ted Goddard *Pembrokeshire Shipwrecks* Christopher Davies, 1983

D. Hampton & G. Middleton *The Story of the St David's Lifeboat* 1989

Ivor Wynne Jones *Shipwrecks of North Wales* David & Charles, 1973

Brian Luxton *Old Barry in Photographs* Stewart Williams, 1978

Richard McElwee *The Last Voyages of his Waterford Steamers* The Book Centre, Waterford, undated

D. J. Morgan *Disasters in the Bristol Channel: The Great Gale of 1908* article in *Maritime Wales* No 10, 1986

Henry Parry *Wreck and Rescue on the Coast of Wales (The Story of the North Wales Lifeboats)* D. Bradford Barton Ltd, 1973

Vernon Scott *An Experience Shared* Laleham Publications, 1992

Ian Skidmore *Anglesey & Lleyn Shipwrecks* Christopher Davies, 1979

Graham Smith *Smuggling in the Bristol Channel* Countryside Books, 1989

Shipwrecks of the Bristol Channel Countryside Books, 1991

Newspapers: *South Wales Echo, West Wales Guardian, Western Telegraph, The Cambrian and Barry Dock News*

The romantic, perhaps traditional, view of shipwreck and disaster at sea is fairly easy to conjure. Invariably there are towering waves which crash down onto the tiny schooner while sea spray and spume whip viciously through the air. A gallant sailor stands defiantly with matted hair and drenched white shirt, one arm protectively around the shoulders of a terrified woman passenger, the other clinging to the mizzen shrouds. A sense of duty and sacrifice pervades everything — it needs only Alfred Noyes or Rudyard Kipling to start intoning some ponderous Victorian epic and the picture would be complete.

Reality, however, is usually different. Shipwrecks are rarely romantic and, while there is often bravery, sometimes on a quite momentous or heroic scale, it is the tragedy of the occasion which remains long after the events themselves are forgotten or consigned to distant memory. Occasionally there is a strange, perverse humour in the event, a rollicking farce which would have Compton Mackenzie splitting his sides in mirth. Normally, however, it is the drama and the futile waste of life which people remember.

Britain, as an island nation, has always needed the sea, as a defence and as a vital supply link. Never being totally self-sufficient, the need to import raw materials, food items and luxury goods has been paramount. In return, there have always been goods to export. Additionally, during the past hundred or so years, people have increasingly used the sea as a means of leisure-time activity. It is hardly surprising, then, that a small percentage of the sailing craft, oil tankers and cargo vessels which litter the seaways around Britain should have come to grief upon its coastline. Indeed, when you consider the number of ships which have skirted British coasts, in the past as well as the present, the real wonder lies not in the fact there have been so many shipwrecks but, rather, that there have been so few.

Wales, at the western extremity of the kingdom, has invariably born the brunt of the severe weather which batters the British Isles. As such, this tiny and ancient country has had more than its fair share of shipwrecks and maritime disasters. Sailing vessels have always been prone to the vagaries of the weather but the gales and adverse climatic conditions which regularly beset Wales have taken equally as severe a toll on the iron ships and powered vessels of the twentieth century.

Three main areas, broad divisions which are, by their very nature, generalizations, provide the basis for any study of Welsh shipwrecks. These are the North Wales coastline, Pembrokeshire and the South Wales coast which borders the Bristol Channel. The reasons are obvious. All three areas lie on important shipping routes.

The North Wales coast has, for many years, seen vessels, large and small, sweeping in off the Atlantic and Irish Sea, bound for destinations as varied as Holyhead and Caernarvon, Beaumaris and Amlwch. Initially, trade was with Ireland, the continent and with other parts of Britain while the cargoes tended to consist of items such as woollen goods, wine and agricultural produce. In medieval times Beaumaris was the main destination on Anglesey while Chester was the chief port on the English coast.

By the early nineteenth century, however, Liverpool had become the major port in the north of England and maritime traffic was attracted like a magnet towards it. Towns like Flint and Connah's Quay had also increased in both prosperity and importance, thanks largely to the lead and coal mines of the region. Liverpool concentrated its efforts on trade with America, Australia and the more distant parts of the globe. On a daily basis dozens of cargo and passenger ships moved in and out of this sprawling vibrant port, each of them eager to grab its own lucrative share of the business.

The main shipping routes to and from Liverpool (and, for that matter, the North Wales ports) passed close to the rocky shores of Anglesey and the Lleyn Peninsula. Bad weather, poor navigation, ill judgement and sheer bad luck could all combine to bring vessels to disaster on this deadly stretch of coast.

One hundred miles due south, Pembrokeshire stands like a gnarled and knotted fist at the south western edge of Wales. For heavily laden vessels, perhaps beating up from the Azores, running in before an Atlantic storm or simply cruising northwards from Land's End, Pembrokeshire was — and remains — both a landmark and terrible danger. Its rugged cliffs and wide, sweeping beaches lie open to the elements. Woe betide any unwary mariner who approaches them without due care and attention.

Milford Haven, one of the finest natural harbours in the world, provides a sanctuary of sorts but its entry is guarded by a vicious coastline and by high, soaring cliffs. In the days of sailing vessels, to be swept onto this coast before a south-westerly gale meant certain disaster. In more recent years the development of the oil refining industry in the Haven produced added shipping movements, replacing the trade from once thriving ports like Porthgain, Fishguard and Solva. No part of Pembrokeshire is more than twenty five miles from the sea — it remains an important element in the area's economy.

The Bristol Channel has always been a vitally important passageway for maritime trade. One of the earliest routes into Britain from the Mediterranean and continent, it was effectively the key to the western seaboard. Celts, Romans and Vikings all sailed up the estuary. Dozens of strategically placed ports line its banks, on both Welsh and English sides, but there can be no doubt that for many years Bristol was premier among them. Trade with Europe and the Americas brought wealth to Bristol, so much so that it became second only to London in significance. The city can trace its origins back to the eleventh century and it was from here that John and Sebastian Cabot sailed in 1497, hoping to find a way to the Indies across the north Atlantic. They failed but they did discover Newfoundland.

However, during the nineteenth century the importance of Bristol began to decline. As King Coal asserted his insidious power, the Welsh ports — places like Newport, Cardiff, Penarth and Swansea — gradually assumed greater significance. This meant an enormous increase in the amount of shipping in the Bristol Channel, a seaway which is dangerous at the best of times. A long, narrow waterway, it has one of the highest tidal ranges in the world. Flood tides of five to six knots are common — with such a racing tide, backed by severe gales from the south or south west, small wonder that the phrase 'God help sailors on a night like this' achieved such poignancy in relation to the Bristol Channel. The Gower, Cefn Sidan Sands and Nash Point are just three areas on the Welsh coast which easily and quickly became deathtraps during the nineteenth and early twentieth centuries.

The stories of shipwreck and disaster on the Welsh coast are legion. Many of them concern 'wreckers', those unknown bands of callous criminals who supposedly set false lights in order to lure ships onto the rocks. Such tales are probably exaggerated. Deliberately causing shipwrecks was, in most cases, unthinkable and while one or two instances may have happened, the majority of occurrences were probably sheer opportunism. A disaster took place, often with the loss of the total crew, and the local populace simply helped themselves from the wreckage. It was, after all, a frugal life and simple country people had to make a living as best they could.

5

The stories, however, remain fascinating. One of the most famous concerns an old couple living on the coast near Amroth. According to legend they regularly lured vessels on to the rocks below their cottage and enjoyed a lucrative life-style on the proceeds. Their only son, reaching manhood, took up the sea as a career and spent several years away from home. One night, hearing of a vessel beating in from the Atlantic, the old couple set their false lights and settled down in front of the fire as the ship died on the rocks below them. The following morning, gleefully sifting through the debris on the beach, the old man came across the half-drowned body of a sailor, face down at the water's edge. Taking a large stone he quickly smashed in the sailor's skull. There could be no survivors. When he turned the body over, in order to search the dead man's pockets, he was appalled to see the face of his only son. Such tales are probably apocryphal but they are now part of the folklore which surrounds shipwrecks.

As in so many stories from the distant past, it is hard to distinguish fact from fiction. The famous Dollar Ship of the Gower is one case in question. Supposedly wrecked on Rhossili Sands in the seventeenth century, nobody has actually seen the galleon but there are many tales of silver dollars washed up along the beaches of the region. Actual coins are in existence but whether or not they originate from the Dollar Ship is another matter. No official record of the wreck exists although there are many tales, involving murder, ghosts and treasure hunts, surrounding the vessel. It hardly matters. The story is a good one — and it must be remembered that three or four hundred years ago ships could well have foundered, gone down with all hands, on some deserted stretch of coast without anybody on shore knowing anything about the tragedy.

No book on shipwrecks would ever be complete without mention of the rescue services. Amazingly, despite the fact that ships have been trading and sailing around the coast of Britain for thousands of years, it was not until the nineteenth century, with the burgeoning power of the British Empire providing an effective nucleus and impetus, that formal rescue networks were developed.

Premier among these networks, the National Institution for the Preservation of Life from Shipwrecks was founded in 1824. The organization changed its name to to the Royal National Lifeboat Institution in 1854 and soon a network of lifeboats, each manned by a volunteer crew, sprang up around the coast of Britain. The RNLI, its history and developing role, is too well known to require much detailed documentation here. Suffice it to say that it has given, and continues to give, invaluable aid to shipwreck and endangered sailors. Without the RNLI the toll of dead seamen would be far, far greater.

In 1836 Trinity House was given the right to control all lights marking reefs and dangerous rocks around the coast. Prior to this, lights had existed but they were usually privately owned. This was a lucrative business, as Ted Goddard commented about the Smalls Lighthouse off the Pembrokeshire Coast:

'When Trinity House was empowered to take control of all lights in 1836, they had to pay its owner £170,000 in compensation. (*Pembrokeshire Shipwrecks*)

Often, the style of operation for these early lighthouses was, to say the least, bizarre. The light at Point Lynas on Anglesey, established in 1781, was no more than the upper floor of an ordinary house. Every evening the windows on the upper floor were illuminated — a system which worked until 1 August 1835, when a new lighthouse went into operation on the same spot.

On 15 January 1822 the operational forces of the Customs and Excise departments (Revenue cutters, the Preventive Waterguard and the riding officers) were amalgamated into the Coast Guard, the name originally spelt as two words. Originally under the direction of the Customs Board, from 1831 the new service became virtually a Naval Reserve. While for several years the main purpose of the Coastguard remained the apprehension of smugglers, the heady days of smuggling runs and smuggling gangs were over by the middle decades of the nineteenth century. Thereafter, the Coastguard began to concentrate more on coast watching and life preservation. Coastguards' duties now include alerting rescue services and, if necessary, effecting rescues themselves.

At the end of the nineteenth century lifesaving apparatus companies were founded. Manned by local volunteers, these companies used rockets to carry lines from shore to stranded ships. As early as 1819 a number of the Preventive Waterguard units of the Customs Service had been equipped with Manby's Mortar, an early but cumbersome rocket system. By 1825 all Coastguard stations were using these rockets. The lifesaving companies, at the end of the century, used the lighter Boxer rockets, which superseded Manby's Mortars, and volunteer units existed at various places along the Welsh coast. The process of rescue from the shore was a sound one which continued in use well into the twentieth century. The wreck of the *Samtampa* in 1947 is just one example when rockets were used to attempt rescue, albeit without success.

So much, then, for rescue provision. As the nineteenth century unfolded, Wales, like other maritime areas of Britain, became reasonably well provided with such services. Yet when disaster struck it hardly mattered what provision was available; lifeboat, lifesaving companies, Coastguard and Trinity House — it was literally every hand to the helm. At the end of the day it invariably came down to individual skill, individual bravery and, often, sheer luck!

No book like this can ever attempt to be a definitive history of Welsh shipwrecks. It is, at best, a representative selection. Some of the wrecks presented here are well known; others are described for perhaps the first time. There are many more which are not touched upon at all. Literally thousands of shipping disasters must have occurred around the Welsh coast over the years — a large number of them unrecorded and unnoticed; others live on in folklore and legend. Therein perhaps lies part of the fascination for shipwrecks, the sense of tapping into unknown information, of trying to separate fact from fiction.

By its very title — *Welsh Shipwrecks in Camera* — this book limits itself largely to the last hundred or so years. With the exception of a few early prints, the examples of shipwreck presented here come from the age of photographs and picture postcards. Photography is a fairly recent innovation but there can be no doubt that it has revolutionized the study of history. It is a misnomer to say that these photographs, or any others for that matter, can ever stand totally alone but, by their immediacy, their accuracy and their sheer poignancy these views seem to catch perfectly the mood and feel of each individual tragedy.

And yet, despite this, studying them now, many years after the events they so faithfully record, there is a sense of objectivity about the photographs — objectivity which is quite remarkable. It is also necessary. As the poet Philip Larkin once said about Gerard Manley Hopkins' famous poem *The Wreck of the Deutschland*, it would have been 'markedly inferior if Hopkins had been a survivor from the passenger list'.

Hindsight then, like objectivity, is surely one of the few exact sciences!

This classic early postcard shows the coaster 'Morray Firth' which ran ashore at Llandulas, North Wales, in 1907. The message on the reverse reads 'This shows a boat which recently got into trouble on the beach'. Obviously the 'Morray Firth' sustained only limited damage. (PC)

A somewhat romanticised impression of the lifeboat service, this shows the Llandudno boat setting out on a rescue mission. Nevertheless, with the tiny vessel pounded by breakers and heavy seas, it does give a good indication of the conditions lifeboatmen have to endure. (PC)

The schooner 'Flying Foam' was wrecked on the western side of the Great Orme on 21 June 1936. Carrying a cargo of coal, it was seriously damaged and the crew rescued by Beaumaris lifeboat. Some cargo was saved, however, as can be seen in this photograph where carts are being loaded with coal the following day. (GAS)

The 'Rothsay Castle' was lost in August 1831 on Dutchman's Bank at the mouth of the Menai Straits. One of Britain's first steam-driven ships, she was intended to work the River Clyde but by 1831 was worn out. Brought south from the Clyde by Liverpool businessman Thomas Watson, three of her crew paid themselves off during the journey, so unseaworthy was she. (NMM)

The 'Rothsay Castle' was dangerously over-loaded with day trippers bound for Beaumaris. A heavy sea was running and water poured in through her seams, yet the captain refused to turn back. She ran onto Dutchman's Bank at low water; the ship repeatedly smashed onto the sandbank. Panic spread quickly and in the ensuing confusion there were only 23 survivors. (NMM)

HMS 'Thetis' was lost in Liverpool Bay, 15 miles east of Llandudno, in 1939. The newly completed vessel left the builder's yard for diving trials on 31 June, carrying a crew of 55 and an additional 50 dockyard technicians. She failed to rise from her first dive — water flooded through a torpedo tube into forward compartments. Four of the trapped men were able to escape using Davis apparatus and for a while her stern protruded above sea but at 3.00 pm on 1 July she slid below the surface. Everybody on board subsequently died. (GAS)

Four months after the disaster, with war declared against Germany and submarines in desperately short supply, 'Thetis' was raised and beached for repairs at Traeth Bychan near Moelfre. The bodies of the dead were removed and the vessel renamed 'Thunderbolt'. She served in the RN until 1943 when she was sunk by enemy action off Sicily.
(JR)

14

A training ship known as 'Conway' had served on the Mersey and in the Menai Straits since 1859. The last vessel to bear the name was wrecked in 1953. During her career as a TS the 'Conway' (three different vessels) prepared thousands of boys for careers at sea. Originally a 90 gun battleship called 'Nile', the wrecked vessel had been in service as a TS since 1875. (JR)

On 14 April 1953 'Conway' ws towed from her moorings by two tugs, 'Dongarth' and 'Minegarth', bound for Cammell Laird's dry dock at Birkenhead and a much needed refit. Between the Britannia Railway Bridge and Menai Suspension Bridge, the tow line parted and 'Conway' ran ashore on the Caernarvonshire side. Badly damaged, her compartments flooded, the old woodenwall was declared a total loss. (JR)

The loss of the 'Royal Charter' on Tuesday 25 October 1859 was one of the worst disasters to hit the Welsh coast. Returning from Australia with 324 passengers (many of them successful gold prospectors), a cargo of wood, sheepskins and half a million pounds in gold, she was forced onto the rocks at Point Lynas. Broadside on to pounding sixty foot waves, she lay just yards from safety while villagers from Moelfre watched helplessly. Over 450 people died in a mad half-hour of panic. (GAS)

The Moelfre lifeboat 'Star of Hope', a self-righting vessel built in 1892, is here under sail and oar propulsion. She was on station at Moelfre until 1910 when she went out of RNLI service. The Moelfre lifeboat was, for many years, a vitally important link in the rescue services on the North Wales coast. (IB)

This rare photograph shows the Mersey ferry 'Pansy' ashore on the rocks at Bull Bay on Anglesey. Built in 1896 for the Wallasy Corporation, 'Pansy' was 180 ft long and had a gross tonnage of 333 tons. In 1916 she was requisitioned for war service but, while on the way to London, was wrecked in Bull Bay. (JR)

The 1,130 ton iron steamer 'Olinda' was wrecked due to pilot's error, on Harry Furlong's Reef off Anglesey on 26 January 1854. Built nine months earlier, she was outward bound for South America, with a cargo worth over £50,000. After striking the rocks on her port side the force of the tide swung the vessel around so that she was subsequently holed on both sides. Passengers and crew were taken off by the Cemlyn Bay lifeboat. (GAS)

The South Stack lighthouse at Holyhead was one of many lights erected on the North Wales coast. The lighthouse became an important landmark for sailors bound to and from Liverpool and Holyhead harbour. (PC)

'Primrose Hill' was a 2,520 ton barque, wrecked on 28 December 1900, close to South Stack lighthouse. Towed from the Mersey on Christmas Eve, she lost her tow line off Bardsey Island during the night of 27/28 December. The LNWR steamer 'Hibernia' attempted rescue but her own steering gear broke during the operation. 'Primrose Hill', dragging her anchors in a rising gale, struck a submerged rock and broke up in five minutes with the loss of all but one of her crew. Twelve apprentices were among the dead. (JR)

This early print (c1854) shows an attempted rescue on the Welsh coast near Aberystwyth. An unknown ship is in danger out in the bay and local seamen are attempting to launch a fishing boat to go to her aid. In the days before the establishment of the lifeboat service, many rescues were successfully carried out by local fishermen and sailors. (PC)

This later postcard view by Scott Russell and Co shows the launch of the Aberystwyth lifeboat (c1905). Cardigan Bay, while not on the main shipping routes, saw a considerable amount of local traffic and the services of the rescue organizations were often called for on this wild and windswept coast. (PC) OPPOSITE: The Irish Sea proved to be something of a graveyard for both working and cargo vessels in the years of the Great War. U62 sank two steamers of the Clyde Shipping Company, the 'Formby' and the 'Coningsberg' on the nights of 15 and 17 December 1917. This drawing shows the 'Formby' at sea. (AM)

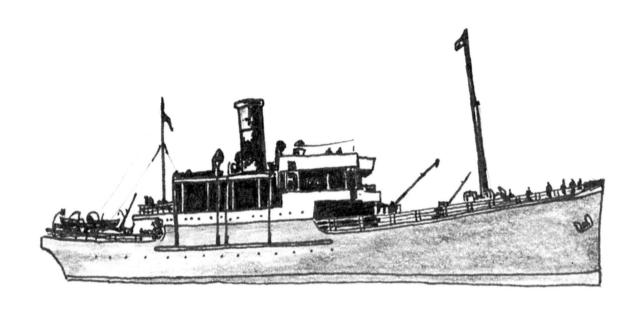

SS 'Coningberg' is shown here in peaceful days before the war. There were no survivors from either attack and no warnings were given. In all, 83 passengers and crew lost their lives, 67 of them from the Waterford area of Ireland. Both ships broke up and sank within minutes of the torpedoes striking. (AMC)

The 'Albatross', a small trading vessel, was wrecked on Llangranog beach in 1912. In this earlier view she is seen moored off the same beach. Look at the bathing tents and, at the left of the picture, what appears to be a tea tent — local entrepreneurs at work? (WIMM)

The liner Herefordshire, battered by waves on the Cardigan Island coast, where she ran on the rocks after breaking adrift from tugs taking her to the Clyde to be broken up. Her skeleton crew of four lashed themselves to a rope and escaped to the island, from which they were rescued by breeches buoy.

LEFT: Wrecked on Cardigan Island in 1934 the liner 'Herefordshire' provided great local interest. On her way to the Clyde for scrapping, she broke free from her tugs and ran onto the island. (WIMM) RIGHT: A newspaper cutting shows the 'Herefordshire' on Cardigan Island. Her skeleton crew of four had lashed themselves to a rope, crossed to the island and later escaped to the mainland by breeches buoy. The wreck was bought by Captain W. G. James of Ivy House, Llangranog. (WIMM)

The 'Drumloch', a small coaster which plied the shoal waters of Cardigan Bay, is here grounded on a sand bar in the Teifi River. Waiting for the tide to turn, the crew spent the period imbibing freely in The Sloop at Porthgain. Consequently, when the time came to cast off, they were far from sober. Thus the 'Drumloch' ran onto the bar at the approach to Cardigan — quite how they managed the twenty mile trip from Porthgain is not recorded! (WIMM)

"DESDEMONA" STRANDED NEWPORT BAY PEM.
11.2.06 AUG DAVIES PHOTO.

30   *The 'Desdemona' became stranded at Newport in the north of Pembrokeshire on 11 February 1906. This photograph shows her ashore on the beach; it was taken by an early pioneer in Pembrokeshire, Aug Davies. (KD)*

LEFT: On 18 November 1893 the Norwegian barque 'Evviva' went ashore in Fishguard Bay. Huge seas were running and the ship was blown helplessly around the bay, striking the rocks below the old Fishguard Fort. A fifteen year old boy was lost overboard before she was smashed to pieces. The skipper, Captain H. Bauhn, and the rest of the crew were saved by the use of rocket apparatus. (WIMM) RIGHT: The rugged rocks and cliffs of Pembrokeshire — a deathtrap for the unwary and uncaring. (PC)

Making passage to Tripoli the cattle freighter 'El Tambo' caught fire in February 1977 and was towed into Fishguard Harbour. The fire was extinguished but legal wrangles kept the vessel anchored for six weeks. Suddenly, on 27 March 1977, she began to settle by the bows and sank. Salvage attempts failed, the ship sinking for a second time when she was brought to the surface. It was not until 1980 that her remains were finally taken away. (RAF)

The Austro-Hungarian steamer 'Szent Istvan' was wrecked on Ramsey Island on 28 September 1908. Bound for Glasgow with a cargo of flour, she ran ashore in a dense fog. Ramsey farmer and coxswain of the St David's lifeboat, Ivor Arnold, cared for the crew who had escaped in four boats. The hull of the ship remained above water for over a week but conditions were too hazardous for anyone to attempt salvage. However, the flour was washed ashore and local people gleefully helped themselves. (PC)

The Greek steamer 'Emmanuel', bound from Manchester to the Mumbles, ran onto rocks in Ramsey Sound in March 1925. Caught off Skokholm Island in a violent storm her Captain decided to seek shelter in St Brides Bay. However, 'Emmanuel', in ballast, was light and unmanageable and refused to make headway. As a result it was decided to run before the wind and head for the Fishguard area. (LB)

'Emmanuel' had reached the North Bishops when the wind changed and she was unable to round the rocks. The skipper tried to take her through Ramsey Sound. Midway through, caught by wind and tide, she went ashore. St David's lifeboat and the lifesaving apparatus company were involved in the rescue, some of the crew being stranded on a small reef between wreck and land. A local man, David Edwards, gave valuable assistance. He was never given recognition — possibly because of harsh words he later said about the rescue services. (PC)

'Emmanuel's' troubles were not over. During rescue operations to pull her off the rocks she ran onto the steam trawler 'William Cale' and nearly drove her ashore. Towed into Milford Haven for repair she then collided with another trawler, the 'Arthur Cavanagh'. At the subsequent inquiry the crew of 'Emmanuel' were cleared of blame. This unusual photograph shows her in dry dock: inside the hull is a workman. (KD)

Lifeboats had been stationed at St David's since 1869. The 'Gem' arrived in 1885, a twelve-oared sailing and pulling boat. On 12 October 1910, under Coxswain John Stephens, she set out to assist the ketch 'Democrat' which had got into difficulties in Ramsey Sound. A heavy sea was running but the 'hurricane' that many accounts describe is unlikely. Three crewmen were taken off. When trying to manoeuvre through the Bitches 'Gem' hit the rocks and turned over. Coxswain Stephens, Henry Rowlands and James Price were lost. Fifteen men managed to reach the Bitches. (RNLI)

Rescue of 'Gem' was made the following day by two local boats. Sydney Mortimer, later the youngest lifeboat coxswain in Britain, skippered one, achieving deserved fame for his courage and skill. The second boat, crewed by Eleazer James, the brothers Ivor and Adrian Arnold and two others, both called John Davies, has never had full recognition. The local Lifeboat Committee was aware of the part it played, however, stating that it wished 'to express its highest admiration of, and its heartfelt gratitude to, the crews of the two boats who bravely went to the rescue of our wrecked lifeboatmen on the morning of 13th October'. This photograph shows some of the survivors. (PCL)

This shows the 'Vernicos Alexia' and the stern of 'Vernicos Georges', which, together with 'Vernicos Barbara IV', were wrecked near Solva in Pembrokeshire on 18 October 1981. Bought by the Vernicos Company (from the Alexandra Towing Company of Liverpool) the three tugs were en route for Greece, the 'Vernicos Georges' towing the other two, when the lead vessel developed engine trouble. The rope then fouled her propellor and, drifting helplessly, all three vessels went ashore just west of Solva. The crews were rescued by lifeboat and helicopters from RAF Brawdy. (WT)

The oil industry brought prosperity to Milford Haven. It also brought shipwreck. The 'Dona Marika', an 11,000 ton Liberian-registered tanker, was anchored in Dale Roads, waiting to enter the Haven when, on 5 August 1973, she began to drag her anchors. Driven ashore close to St Ishmaels, for a while there was a fear of major disaster. High octane fuel poured into the sea from a gash in the tanker's side and desperate measures were needed from the Conservancy Board, Angle lifeboat and HM Coastguard. It was November before 'Dona Marika' was finally refloated. (WT)

The Great Western steamer 'Roebuck' caught fire on 26 January 1905, while laid up for the winter at Neyland. The GWR fire brigade pumped in so much water that the ship listed to port, the tide ran up and the 'Roebuck' sank at her moorings. With the help of men from Pembroke Dockyard she was raised and taken away for repair. Always an unlucky ship, 'Roebuck' was later requisitioned by the Admiralty, renamed 'Roedean' and sunk by a mine off the Orkneys in 1915. (PC)

A shipwreck which took place before the vessel hit the water, the 'Caesar' was cursed by a witch on the day of her launch! Due for launching from Pembroke Dockyard on 21 July 1853, virtually the whole population came to witness the event. Betty Foggy, a supposed local witch, was refused entry to the yards and cursed the ship, saying 'There will be no launch today'. When the time came 'Caesar' refused to move. Somebody had ordered fir instead of oak for the launching ways and the ship bedded herself into the wood. Betty Foggy's curse was a convenient excuse! (PC)

Bentlass, on Pembroke River, was the scene of a ferry boat disaster in February 1889. In this seemingly innocuous photograph the river looks mild and calm. On the day of the disaster, with a wild west wind blowing, it was a place of sheer menace. Fourteen women, the ferryman and his young assistant were all drowned when one of the passengers panicked, leapt to her feet and the small ferry boat was swamped. (PC)

Thorne Island, one of the original defensive forts for Pembroke Dockyard, was the scene of a Welsh 'Whiskey Galore'
in 1894. Bound for Adelaide with a cargo of 100° proof whisky and gunpowder, 'Loch Shiel' ran ashore on the rocks
of the island on the night of 30 January. A heavy sea was running and it soon became clear that the pumps could not
keep out the water. A mattress soaked in paraffin was lit on deck as a distress signal and the Angle lifeboat took off
passengers and crew. (PC)

The real story of the 'Loch Shiel', however, was just beginning. As the ship began to break up the cargo floated inland. Despite the rapid appearance of Customs officers, most of the whisky was spirited away by locals and hidden in gardens, houses and attics. Bottles were concealed down the legs of women's bloomers and cases boarded up in alcoves. Three men died, two of them drowned trying to recover whisky, the other from alcohol poisoning, but it could easily have been many more — several locals carried home cases of gunpowder, thinking they were whisky! (TG)

Freshwater West was the scene of tragedy in 1943 when LCGs (Landing Craft Guns) 15 and 16 sank just a few hundred yards off the beach. Bound for Falmouth the two unwieldy craft encountered deteriorating weather in Cardigan Bay. Refused permission to seek shelter in Fishguard or Milford Haven they ploughed on until they were overwhelmed by mountainous seas. LCG 15 sank within sight of hundreds of watchers on the beach, the marines on board drowned or smashed to death on the rocks. LCG 16 foundered later in the night. (PC)

46

The sloop 'Rosemary' was one of several vessels which attempted rescue but she was unable to get a line across to LCG 16. Six sailors volunteered to take the line in a whaler but it, too, was swamped and the sailors drowned. There were only three survivors in the worst wartime disaster of its type in Britain, made all the more poignant because it need never have happened had the densely packed vessels been allowed into either Fishguard or Milford Haven. (TG)

Freshwater West was the graveyard of many ships. This shows the keel of an unknown vessel on the beach, taken in June 1990 after violent storms had removed much of the sand. It is possible that it is the keel of a Portuguese brig, 'Gram Para', which hit the beach in a dense fog on 7 May 1855, spewing its cargo of india rubber and nuts along the coast, and becoming a total wreck. There is no definite proof. (JVR)

On 20 August 1906, the 'Princess Irene', en route for Bristol from Aberdeen, ran into dense fog off the Pembrokeshire coast. Thinking the entrance to the Bristol Channel was near, her captain set a course towards St Govans Head. Instead of passing to the south of the headland, the vessel drove straight onto Linney Head. All of the crew were saved and various goods salvaged but 'Princess Irene' had broken her back and became a total wreck. (PC)

Another unknown vessel here drives ashore on St Govans Head. There are several possibilities for this wreck — perhaps the 'Annie Park' or 'Neptune'. More probably it is the 78-ton ketch 'Florrie', wrecked on 2 July 1918, bound for Cardiff with a cargo of burnt ore. There is no clear answer but the photograph gives a superb indication of the violence of the sea around the Pembrokeshire coast. (PC)

Since 1907 a lightship had been maintained by Trinity House, three miles off St Govans Head. The vessel in the illustration is the 'St Gowan', Lightship No 10, built around 1949/50 by Phillips and Sons of Dartmouth. The manned lightship off St Govans was replaced by an automated vessel in 1985. (WT)

HMS 'Montague', a Duncan class battleship, went aground on Lundy Island's infamous Shutter Rock at the mouth of the Bristol Channel on 30 May 1906. Launched at Devonport in 1901 the 'Montague' had a complement of 750, was armed with 4 x 12 ins and 12 x 6 ins guns and was the pride of the Channel Fleet. She was no match for Lundy's rugged coastline. (PC)

H.N.S. MONTAGU

Engaged in wireless trials with the Scilly Isles, 'Montague' was off course and enveloped by a dense fog when, at 2.12 am on 30 May, she ploughed onto the rocks of Lundy. Several crew members were injured and, although Captain Adair ordered full astern, 'Montague' refused to budge. The rising tide swung her broadside on, both propellors were lost and a large hole was ripped in her bottom. (PC)

Salvage operations on 'Montague' lasted many months. Naval vessels, photographers and dockyard maties all flocked to the area to witness and help in the rescue work. It was a hopeless task — the ship was paid off on 20 August 1906 and attention concentrated on rescuing items like the 12 ins guns (which cost over £9,000 each). In October heavy seas battered the wreck and her back broke; all work was abandoned. (PC)

The 'Cardiff Trader' went aground at Llanelli in 1914 before the outbreak of war. In this marvellous photograph the vessel sits high and dry on the beach, looking for all the world like a stranded whale. Considering the channel beneath her hull it is amazing that she did not break her back. (WIMM)

The Port Eynon lifeboat 'Janet' is here, complete with crew at practice. Stationed at Port Eynon from 1906 until 1916, she later went on to serve at Stornoway until 1924. The first Port Eynon lifeboat was named 'A Daughter's Offering' in 1884 but the station closed in 1916. (IB)

LEFT: Launched on a false call, the Port Eynon boat lost three crew members on 1 January 1916. Broadside on to the wind she was caught by a wave and capsized. Though she righted herself Coxswain Billy Gibbs and lifeboatmen Bill Eynon and George Harry had vanished. This card shows their memorial. (PC) RIGHT: Culver Hole near Port Eynon has been a pigeon house and a smuggler's den. Stories of wreckers setting their lights in the windows of the strange building, built into the cliffs, are grossly exaggerated. (PC)

This dramatic photograph shows the trawler 'Roche Castle' being pounded by the sea several miles west of Swansea on the Gower. Returning to port with a full catch of fish the trawler smashed onto the coast in a dense fog on 10 January 1937. The crew escaped by breeches buoy although one man was drowned when he fell into the sea during the rescue attempt. (AH)

This strange looking structure is not a portion of seawall or a boat house, but the remains of a Hunt Class destroyer, the 'Cleveland', which was wrecked near Burry Holmes on the Gower. Laid up for scrapping, she was being towed to Llanelli by the tug 'Brynforth' when, on 28 June 1957, the tow parted and she drifted ashore. Many months later 'Cleveland' was still stranded and was broken up where she lay on the beach. Thousands flocked to see the vessel and to watch her gradual dismemberment. (PC)

Mumbles lifeboat station was established in 1835. This postcard shows the launch of the lifeboat 'James Stevens No 12' on Regatta Day, 1900. The 'James Stevens' arrived on station in February 1900 but almost exactly three years later she was caught by a freak wave outside Port Talbot harbour, after answering a call to assist the SS 'Christine'. Overturned, the lifeboat righted herself but capsized again almost immediately. Six of the 14 crew were drowned or battered to death on the rocks. (IB)

This 1854 print shows the Mumbles lighthouse and a boat which has been beached for safety on the sands. In 1883 the lighthouse keeper was Abraham Ace. His two daughters, Jennie Ace and Margaret Evans, saved the lives of two lifeboatmen who had been thrown into the sea when the Mumbles lifeboat 'Wolverhampton' overturned during a rescue attempt. By knotting together their shawls as a lifeline, they created a legend which has gone down in story and poem as 'The Women of Mumbles Head'. (PC)

The story of the 'Seaforth' is a little-known tale which took place at Mumbles during World War One. She hit a vessel, the 'Franklin', which had already gone down in the Mumbles Roads, and settled gracefully on the sands. At low tide 'Seaforth' was high and dry. As her rigging appears to be intact (although the funnel seems to have fallen) it is doubtful if she was fully submerged even at high water. (PC)

SS 'Broadland' went aground on Aberavon Beach on 20 January 1913. A Blue Star vessel bound for Punta Arenas in the Magellan Straits, she had just left Port Talbot docks when gusting winds blew her onto the sands. Hundreds of people flocked to watch. A line was carried to the ship by rocket and the first man ashore was a Chinese lamp-room fireman called Chin Gwen. After three hour' hard work all 42 crew were rescued. At low tide 'Broadland' was left high and dry on the beach. (WIMM)

One of the worst gales ever to hit South Wales blew up at the end of Augsut 1908. At midday on 31 August the 'Amazon' anchored to the east of the Mumbles. After a rough, uncomfortable night, a sudden squall hit the ship at about 6.00 am and the starboard cable ran out. Then the port one parted. Hastily raised sails were destroyed by the wind. Forced eastwards, the 'Amazon' struck Margam Sands at 8.00 am, an hour before high water. She struck bow on, then swung around broadside to the waves. (RE/CE)

The fore, main and mizzen masts of 'Amazon' were carried away and huge seas crashed over the vessel. Several men tried to swim ashore but most were snatched away by the sea. The Port Talbot Lifesaving Company arrived on the scene at approximately 9.15 am. By then only two men were left alive. A line was passed to 'Amazon' but the huge seas prevented either man coming ashore. Only when the tide ebbed could they use the line. Twenty one of the crew were drowned, including Captain Garrick and five apprentices. (RE/CE)

The 'Samtampa' wreck lives on in the history of South Wales as one of its worst disasters. On 23 April 1947 the Liberty ship was in ballast and running up the Channel before a south-westerly Force 8 gale. By early evening disaster was imminent — riding high out of the water, 'Samtampa' was blown towards the Welsh coast. Both anchors were out but nothing could stop the doomed vessel. Shortly after 7.00 pm she was hurled onto the rocks of Sker Point, just west of Porthcawl. (MLS)

This rare photograph shows wreckage of 'Samtampa' strewn along the coast on the day after the disaster. Pounded by gigantic breakers the ship broke her back almost as soon as she hit the rocks. The bow section drifted several hundred yards out to sea before it, too, broke in half. The Porthcawl Lifesaving Company tried to reach the wreck with rockets but the wind was too strong. Members of the crew huddled on the stern section but they were beyond help. All 39 men on board died. (AW)

LEFT: The tragedy of the 'Samtampa' was even more appalling because the Mumbles lifeboat 'Edward Prince of Wales' went down with her. Coxswain William Gammon bravely took his tiny vessel out into a sea which had been whipped up by winds of over 70 knots. Not equipped with radio, the lifeboat searched tirelessly for the doomed freighter. The small craft was last seen at 7.10 pm on 23 April. (MLS) RIGHT: It was not until the following day that anybody realized 'Edward Prince of Wales' was missing. The upturned hull was found half a mile along the beach; William Gammon and seven crew had perished trying to help the 'Samtampa'. (MLS)

This postcard view shows 'Camp Barthant', wrecked on Nash Point in June 1918. The wreck was bought by local firm Browns, and a few wagonloads of teak and oak were removed before she was smashed to pieces in a bad storm. The name 'Camp Barthant' may well be a mistake — the owner of Browns always referred to the ship as 'Camberant'. (PC)

The same storm which destroyed the 'Amazon' in August/September 1908 brought disaster to the 'Verajean'. The three-masted sailing ship left Cardiff on 29 August and headed down Channel under tow. Due to a misunderstanding, the two tugs slipped their tow lines on 31 August, near Lundy Island. Captain Ritchie of the 'Verajean' decided the weather was so bad he would return to Barry Docks rather than battle out to the open sea. (PC)

On 1 September, with the wind at hurricane force, the 'Verajean' tried to drop anchor to the east of Nash Point. Both anchor cables ran out to their full length and were lost overboard. Captain Ritchie ordered sails to be set but the wind simply blew them away. Drifting helplessly, 'Verajean' grounded on Rhoose Point. All the crew came ashore but the ship was badly holed and, after ten days on the rocks, was eventually towed to Briton Ferry for breaking. (PC)

The Italian steamship 'Velsesia' hit Friar's Point near Barry Island on 25 August 1926. As the tide receded, the ship settled on the rocks and broke her back. Thousands of holiday-makers flocked to Barry Island to pilfer the cargo, much of which was spread along the beach. Others came to witness the spectacle. 'Valsesia' soon became a major tourist attraction. (PC)

Wreck of the S.S. Valsesia on Friar's Point, Barry Island, 25/8/26.

The 'Valsesia' was carrying coal from South America to Barry when she struck Friar's Point. The miners had been on strike since early in the year and they undoubtedly saw a degree of poetic justice in the wreck! Several attempts were made to salvage the ship but it was March 1927 before Wards of Briton Ferry (who had bought the wreck for £6,600) were able to tow away the two halves. (PC)

*At first sight these two photographs appear the same. In fact they are two different wrecks. ABOVE: The 'Cambo',
a French vessel carrying pit props, ran into the eastern breakwater of Barry Docks on 28 August 1912. Dragged off
by tugs she was beached near the western breakwater but later caught fire and sank in 20 ft of water. On 13 September
she was refloated and towed away for repair. (PC) BELOW: The 'Bizkargi-Mendi', built in 1910, sank off Barry
Docks on 15 March 1911. Once again the shallow depth of water outside the docks can be clearly seen. (WIMM)*

1910.

The 'Walkure', a German cargo ship from Hamburg, was loading bunkers under No 28 tip on Dock 2 at Barry when this accident happened on Thursday 13 August 1908. En route from the Baltic to Natal in Southern Africa with a cargo of deal, she had called at Barry to re-fuel. (PC)

As coal ws tipped into the hold of 'Walkure', she suddenly lurched to port, spilling her deck cargo into the dock. Presumably poor distribtion of coal had caused the list. Fortunately for the German vessel, as she heeled over, her masts caught on the side of the steamer 'Trevessa' and prevented a total capsize. (LB)

The SS 'Pilton' was stranded near Sully Island, close to Penarth, on 27 December 1924. She went ashore on a high tide and was left completely exposed when the tide ran out — an ideal tourist attraction for the people of South Wales. It took five months to effectively and safely refloat her. (PC)

The tanker 'Tafelberg' was mined in the Bristol Channel in 1944. The vessel broke into two halves, both sections beached on the coast. However, with the war against Hitler still raging, merchant ships were in great demand and the two halves were towed into Cardiff docks and welded together. (WIMM)

This view of the re-constructed 'Tafelberg' speaks volumes of the quality of work in Cardiff docks — and you can't even see the join! Sadly, the 'Tafelberg' did not survive. Renamed and fitted out with a new crew she was torpedoed and lost off Scotland before the year was out. (WIMM)

Index to Illustrations